AMERICAN HEROES

CHIEF CRAZY HORSE

Following a Vision

AMERICAN HEROES

CHIEF CRAZY HORSE

Following a Vision

LARRY DANE BRIMNER

Marshall Cavendish
Benchmark
New York

For my sharp-eyed editor, Joyce Stanton,
with thanks

Marshall Cavendish Benchmark
99 White Plains Road
Tarrytown, New York 10591
www.marshallcavendish.us

Library of Congress Cataloging-in-Publication Data
Brimner, Larry Dane.
Chief Crazy Horse : following a vision / by Larry Dane Brimner.
p. cm.
Summary: "A juvenile biography of Crazy Horse, warrior chief of the Oglala tribe of the Sioux nation"
—Provided by publisher.
Includes bibliographical references and index.
ISBN 978-0-7614-3061-2
1. Crazy Horse, ca. 1842–1877—Juvenile literature. 2. Oglala Indians—Kings and rulers—Biography—
Juvenile literature. 3. Oglala Indians—History—Juvenile literature. I. Title.
E99.O3C7218 2009
978.004′9752440092—dc22
[B]
2008002868

Editor: Joyce Stanton   Designer: Anne Scatto
Publisher: Michelle Bisson   Map by Rodica Prato
Art Director: Anahid Hamparian   Printed in Malaysia
                                 135642

Images provided by Debbie Needleman, Picture Researcher, Portsmouth, NH, from the following sources: *Front cover:* Portrait of Crazy Horse, 1876 (oil on canvas) by Henry H. Cross (1837–1918). © Chicago History Museum, USA/The Bridgeman Art Library. *Back cover:* Private Collection/The Bridgeman Art Library/Getty Images. *Pages i, 34:* Portrait of Crazy Horse, 1876 (oil on canvas) by Henry H. Cross (1837–1918). Chicago History Museum, USA/The Bridgeman Art Library; *page ii:* Symbolic portrayal of the conflict between General Custer and Crazy Horse (pigment on canvas) by Kills Two (Nupa Kte), b. 1869. Private Collection/The Stapleton Collection/The Bridgeman Art Library; *p. vi:* Herbert Orth/Time & Life Pictures/Getty Images; *page 3:* Herd of Bison on the Upper Missouri. Plate 40 from Volume 2 of "Travels in the Interior of North America," engraved by William James Bishop (1805-88) and Sigismond Himely (1801–72), 1844 (aquatint) by Karl Bodmer (1809–93) (after). Private Collection/The Stapleton Collection/The Bridgeman Art Library; *page 5:* Bettmann/CORBIS; *page 7:* Fort Laramie. 1858–60(w/c on paper) by Alfred Jacob Miller (1810–74). © Walters Art Museum, Baltimore, USA/The Bridgeman Art Library; *page 9:* Smithsonian American Art Museum, Washington, D.C./Art Resource, NY; *page 11:* Denver Public Library, Western History Collection, Frank A. Rinehart, X-31522; *page 12:* The Lookout (oil on board) by Charles Marion Russell (1865-1926). Private Collection/The Bridgeman Art Library; *pages 15, 31:* MPI/Hulton Archive/Getty Images; *pages 16, 21:* Stock Montage; *page 23:* Denver Public Library. Western History Collection, Joseph Kosseth Dixon photographs, Z-3189; *page 25:* Courtesy Sid Richardson Museum, Fort Worth, Texas/Herbert M. Herget, artist; *page 26:* The Granger Collection, New York; *page 29:* © Stapleton Collection/CORBIS; *page 33:* Denver Public Library, Western History Collection, X-33723

CONTENTS

Chief Crazy Horse
1

Important Dates
34

Words to Know
36

To Learn More about Chief Crazy Horse
38

Index
40

Crazy Horse's tribe got almost everything it needed by following and hunting the buffalo.

Chief Crazy Horse

Chief Crazy Horse was a Native American leader and warrior. He belonged to the Oglala tribe of Sioux Indians. The Oglala hunted the buffalo herds that roamed the northern Great Plains in the American West. The buffalo provided them with almost everything they needed—food, clothing, and shelter.

Crazy Horse was born in the shadow of the Black Hills, near present-day Rapid City, South Dakota. As a child, he was called Curly Hair, or Curly, because of his curly, light brown hair. He would not earn his grown-up name until he was older and performed a brave deed or had a memorable dream.

No one is certain of the exact date of Curly's birth, but most likely it was in 1841. At that time, white settlers were rolling west in the first wagon trains.

Crazy Horse was born near the Black Hills in present-day South Dakota.

At first, the Sioux were merely curious about the strange white folk in their awkward wagons. By the time Curly was ten years old, though, the tide of settlers had swelled. Their endless stream on the Oregon Trail was driving away the buffalo. The Sioux began attacking the settlers to turn them back.

The settlers rolled west in what seemed to be an endless stream of wagons.

In 1851, Curly joined his family and more than ten thousand other Native Americans near Fort Laramie. They had been called there to sign a peace treaty with the United States. The United States promised to give the tribes goods and money. In return, Native Americans agreed to stop attacking the settlers who were passing through their lands. They also agreed to move to reservations.

Curly's family and thousands of other Plains Indians met at Fort Laramie to sign a treaty with the United States.

The treaty, however, was unworkable. Reservation boundaries made no sense to the Sioux. They were not farmers, used to living a settled life. The Sioux were hunters who followed the great buffalo herds. Also, the United States failed to keep its part of the bargain. Some tribes never received the goods and payments that they had been promised. After a short peace, violence erupted again.

The Sioux were not used to living on reservations, and the treaty soon failed.

At age thirteen, Curly was visiting relatives in a nearby village when a young warrior there shot a settler's runaway cow for food. Chief Conquering Bear, the respected leader of the village, tried to work things out by offering to pay the settler for the cow. However, Second Lieutenant John L. Grattan wanted the warrior turned over to the U.S. Army. Conquering Bear refused, and Grattan's soldiers opened fire on the village. Conquering Bear was wounded in the attack and later died.

Chief Conquering Bear was a wise and respected leader.

Curly returned to the village to find dozens of his people dead or dying.

The very next summer, General William S. Harney attacked the village. Curly was visiting again, but he was out chasing wild horses at the time of the attack. When he returned to the village, he found it destroyed. Dozens of his people lay dead.

The two attacks filled Curly with bitterness.

Just after the Grattan fight, Curly had a powerful vision—a dream—about a rider on a horse. That dream would guide his future.

He was seventeen before he tested the vision. He and some other young warriors set out to steal horses from an enemy village. (This was how young warriors learned their fighting skills.) Like the rider in his dream, Curly wore his hair long and unbraided, with a single hawk's feather in it. He tied a small stone behind one ear. He painted only a few hail spots on his body and a red lightning bolt on his cheek.

Like the rider in his dream, Curly wore his hair long and unbraided, with a single hawk's feather in it.

Curly's father proclaimed his son's new name to the entire village.

He found that when he trusted the vision, his enemy's arrows and bullets could not harm him. In the excitement of battle, though, Curly leaped off his horse. He took a scalp—and was struck in the leg by an arrow. He had forgotten his dream's message: *He should never take any war prizes—like scalps—for himself.* He never would again.

Later, his father heard about Curly's brave acts that day. He rewarded his son with his own name: Crazy Horse.

Crazy Horse became a bold and fearless warrior. His enemies said that he was bulletproof.

In 1864, Colonel John M. Chivington and his men attacked a peaceful Cheyenne village in what is southeastern Colorado today. They killed more than 150 Cheyenne, most of them women and children. The attack would come to be called the Sand Creek Massacre.

Runners carried the terrible news to Crazy Horse in his camp near Fort Laramie. The Plains Indians united to seek revenge, and Crazy Horse rode into battle with them. Throughout the winter of 1864–1865, they burned ranches. They attacked wagons and stagecoaches. They tore down telegraph lines. Then they headed farther north, into the wilderness, where there were no settlers and no soldiers in forts.

After the Sand Creek Massacre, Crazy Horse rode into battle to seek revenge.

But soon, miners and prospectors began following the Bozeman Trail north from Fort Laramie to Montana. Soldiers came to protect them, because the Bozeman Trail cut through Sioux territory. Crazy Horse joined with Red Cloud, one of the Sioux leaders, to defend their land. With Crazy Horse and his men acting as decoy, they tricked Captain William J. Fetterman into an ambush. The Sioux called it the Battle of the Hundred Slain. Later, they forced the U.S. Army to abandon the forts it had built along the trail.

Crazy Horse and his men tricked the U.S. Army into an ambush.

By that time, Red Cloud was tired of fighting. He was ready for peace. He led his people onto a reservation and never fought in battle again. But it made no sense to Crazy Horse to give up his freedom. He refused to follow his friend.

Chief Red Cloud, after years of fighting, gave up
and led his people onto a reservation.

For a while, things were quiet. Crazy Horse and his band lived in the northern wilderness as their grandfathers had—chasing buffalo. By 1872, though, the Northern Pacific Railroad was pushing onto land Crazy Horse believed was the Sioux's. He joined up with Chief Sitting Bull, leader of the Hunkpapa tribe of Sioux, to drive off the railroad workers.

Around the same time, he married Black Shawl. Soon after, the couple had a baby daughter, whom they named They-Are-Afraid-of-Her. The happiness the child brought to Crazy Horse's tepee quickly faded, though. They-Are-Afraid-of-Her became ill and died in 1874.

In the northern wilderness, Crazy Horse married Black Shawl,
had a daughter, and lived as the Sioux always had.

*With the discovery of gold in the Black Hills
came miners, then soldiers.*

Other troubles followed. Gold was discovered in the Black Hills, and the U.S. government now wanted to buy the land from the Sioux. The Sioux leaders turned down the offer, so the government decided to take the Black Hills by force. It sent runners to tell the northern tribes to report to a reservation by January 31, 1876, or soldiers would march against them.

The January snow was deep. Many Sioux would die if they moved. The January deadline passed, and the soldiers marched.

By June, General George Crook was closing in on Crazy Horse. But Crazy Horse and Sitting Bull, joined by Cheyenne allies, surprised the general and his troops with a morning attack along Rosebud Creek. This victory cut off reinforcements that might have aided another U.S. Army leader, Colonel George Armstrong Custer.

Custer also was trying to capture Crazy Horse. Later that month, at the Little Bighorn River, Crazy Horse and Sitting Bull defeated Custer. When the Battle of the Little Bighorn was over, Custer and every one of his men lay dead. It was the greatest military victory the Sioux and Cheyenne had ever known.

The Battle of the Little Bighorn was a great victory for the Sioux and their allies.
Crazy Horse's cousin, Amos Bad Heart Bull, drew this picture so that his people would remember.

After defeating Custer, Crazy Horse and Sitting Bull split up. Sitting Bull led his people away to Canada. Crazy Horse held out for a while. But the Oglala were hungry and tired of fighting. He realized that the best way to protect them was to surrender. On May 6, 1877, he surrendered to the U.S. Army and led his people, numbering more than one thousand, onto a reservation. There he was reunited with his old friend Red Cloud. His long struggle to remain free was over.

Chief Sitting Bull, leader of the Hunkpapa tribe of Sioux

What Crazy Horse didn't know, however, was that his time on the reservation would be brief. When he arrived, he was very popular. Everyone wanted to meet the warrior who had defeated Custer. They wanted to know this quiet man who, guided by his dream's message, was famous for his charity to the old and poor.

But all the attention Crazy Horse received made Red Cloud jealous. He spread rumors, and soon Crazy Horse was arrested. When Crazy Horse realized he was being taken to the guardhouse, he struggled to free himself—and was stabbed in the back. He died on September 5, 1877—betrayed by someone he once had called friend.

Crazy Horse's loyal people followed the great warrior on his last march.

IMPORTANT DATES

1841 Crazy Horse (called Curly Hair, or Curly) is born.*

1851 Young Curly and his family attend the Great Fort Laramie Treaty Council with thousands of other Plains Indians.

1854 Curly witnesses the attack on Conquering Bear by the U.S. Army. Has a vision that will guide his future as a warrior.

1855 Returns to his relatives' village to find that it has been destroyed.

1858 His brave deeds on a horse-stealing raid earn him the name Crazy Horse.

1864 Colonel Chivington and his men attack a peaceful Cheyenne village. The attack becomes known as the Sand Creek Massacre.

1866 Crazy Horse and his men trick the troops led by Captain Fetterman into an ambush. The battle becomes known as the Battle of the Hundred Slain.

* Much of what we know about Crazy Horse is uncertain. Accounts of his birth place the year anywhere from 1838 to 1845. Even photographs that claim to be of him are questionable, since it is said that he wouldn't pose for photographs.

1868 Crazy Horse and Red Cloud force the U.S. Army to abandon its forts along the Bozeman Trail. Red Cloud reports to the Sioux Reservation.

1872 Crazy Horse marries Black Shawl. He joins forces with Sitting Bull.

1874 Crazy Horse's daughter, They-Are-Afraid-of-Her, dies.

1875 The U.S. government wants the Black Hills because gold has been discovered there. It orders the Sioux to report to a reservation.

1876 General George Crook is ordered to round up the Sioux and is defeated at Rosebud Creek. Colonel George Armstrong Custer and his troops are wiped out at the Battle of the Little Bighorn—some call it Custer's Last Stand.

1877 On May 6, Crazy Horse surrenders to the U.S. Army. In September, he dies from a stab wound in the back.

WORDS TO KNOW

abandon To leave completely.

allies Groups that associate with one another for a common purpose; friends.

ambush A surprise attack made by people who are in a hidden place.

band A small group of people who live together.

betray To be disloyal.

Bozeman Trail A trail that branched off the Oregon Trail at Fort Laramie and led north to mining camps in Montana.

Cheyenne Native Americans who lived on the Great Plains; friends of the Sioux.

decoy A person who leads another person into danger or into a trap.

Great Plains The vast area of dry grasslands in the United States (and Canada) east of the Rocky Mountains.

guardhouse A building used as a jail.

massacre A brutal, bloody killing of many helpless people.

Oregon Trail The two thousand-mile-long trail across the Great Plains used by white settlers traveling to the American West.

reservation An area of land set aside by the U.S. government for Native Americans to live on.

rumors Stories or gossip, usually untrue.

Sioux Native Americans who lived on the northern Great Plains; the Sioux nation was made up of several independent tribes, among them the Oglala and Hunkpapa.

treaty A written agreement between two or more groups of people.

To Learn More about Chief Crazy Horse

WEB SITES

Encyclopaedia Britannica Concise
> http://concise.britannica.com/ebc/article-9361846/
> Crazy-Horse

Dr. E's Social Science Webzine
> http://emayzine.com/lectures/CRAZYHOR.html

Fact Monster
> http://www.factmonster.com

Indians.org
> http://www.indians.org/welker/crazyhor.htm

BOOKS

Chief Crazy Horse by Chet Cunningham, A&E/Lerner
> Publications Company, 2000.

Crazy Horse by D. L. Birchfield, Raintree Publishers, 2003.

Crazy Horse: Young War Chief by George Edward Stanley, Simon
& Schuster, 2005.

PLACES TO VISIT

Crazy Horse Memorial
12151 Avenue of the Chiefs
Crazy Horse, SD 57730-9506
PHONE: (605) 673-4681 WEB SITE: **http://www.crazyhorse.org**

Little Bighorn Battlefield National Monument
PO Box 39
Exit 510 off I-90 Hwy. 212
Crow Agency, MT 59022-0039
PHONE: (406) 638-3204 WEB SITE: **http://www.nps.gov/libi**

INDEX

Page numbers for illustrations are in boldface.

Army, U.S., 10, **12**, 13, 18, **19**,
    20, **21**, 27-28, 30
attacks
    on Indians, 10, **12**, 13-14,
        18, 27–28
    on settlers, 4, 6, 17, 18

Battle of the Hundred Slain, 20
Battle of Little Bighorn, 28, **29**
Black Hills, South Dakota, 2, **3**,
    26, 27
Black Shawl (wife), 24, **25**
Bozeman Trail, 20
buffalo, 1, 4, 8, 24

Canada, 30
Chivington, Col. John M., 18
Conquering Bear, Chief, 10, **11**
Crazy Horse, Chief, 1, **12**
    and Army attacks, 10, **12**,
        13–14, 18, **19**, 20, **21**,
        22, 28, **29**

in Battle of Little Bighorn, 28,
    29, 30
birth and childhood, 2, **3**, 4,
    6
Crazy Horse name, **16**, 17
death, 32, **33**
marriage and children, 24, **25**
and Red Cloud, 20, **21**, 22,
    30, 32
and Sitting Bull, 24, 28, 30
surrenders to U.S. Army, 30
visions, 14, **15**, 17
Crook, Gen. George, 28
Custer, Col. George Armstrong,
    28, 32

Fetterman, Capt. William J., 20
Fort Laramie, 6, **7**, 18, 20

gold, **26**, 27
Grattan, Lt. John L., 10
Great Plains, 1

Harney, Gen. William S., 13
Hundred Slain, Battle of the, 20

Little Bighorn, Battle of, 28, **29**

miners, 20, **26**

Native Americans
    at Fort Laramie, 6, **7**
    Cheyenne, 18, 28
    discovery of gold and the
        Sioux, **26**, 27
    Plains Indians, 1, **7**, 18
    on reservations, 6, 8, 22, 30
    Sioux Indians, vi, 1, 4, 8, **9**,
        20, 24, 27-28, **29**, 30
Northern Pacific Railroad, 24

Oregon Trail, 4

peace treaties, 6, **7**, 8

Red Cloud, Chief, 20, 22, **23**,
    30, 32
reservations, Indian, 6, 8, 22, 30
Rosebud Creek attack, 28

Sand Creek Massacre, 18
settlers traveling west, 2, **5**
    attacks on, 4, 6
Sitting Bull, Chief, 24, 28, 30,
    31

They-Are-Afraid-of-Her
    (daughter), 24

wagon trains, 2, 4, **5**

ABOUT THE AUTHOR

LARRY DANE BRIMNER is the author of almost 150 books for children, many of them award-winners. Among his fiction and nonfiction titles are *A Migrant Family*, an NCSS/CBC Notable Trade Book in the Field of Social Studies; *The Littlest Wolf*, an IRA/CBC Children's Choice book, Oppenheim Gold Medal recipient, and 2004 Great Lakes' Great Books (Michigan) Honor book; and *Subway: The Story of Tunnels, Tubes, and Tracks*, a Junior Library Guild selection. Larry makes his home in Tucson, Arizona. To learn more about him, investigate his Web site at www.brimner.com.